Celebrated Jazzy Solos

10 Solos in Jazz Syles for Late Elementary Pianists

Robert D. Vandall

MW00813830

Jazz has been a part of my life for as long as I can remember. As a young piano student, I played all of the left-hand boogie patterns in a piano book by Hazel Scott. My father belonged to a record club, and I listened to his recordings of Dave Brubeck, Art Tatum and Errol Garner. When I was older, I bought my own jazz albums featuring Andre Previn and Peter Nero. I became a devoted fan of George Gershwin.

Jazz is irresistible, and pianists of all ages enjoy boogie, blues, ragtime, swing and other jazz idioms. In my *Celebrated Jazzy Solos* series, I wanted to write music that would introduce students to some of the forms, scales, rhythms and harmonies of jazz through its varied styles. It is my hope that they will have fun exploring these pieces and enjoy their journey through the world of jazz.

Best wishes,

Robert D. Vandall

Contents

ISBN-10: 0-7390-6115-1
ISBN-13: 978-0-7390-6115-2

Slide Easy

Robert D. Vandall

Bruce's Boogie

Robert D. Vandall

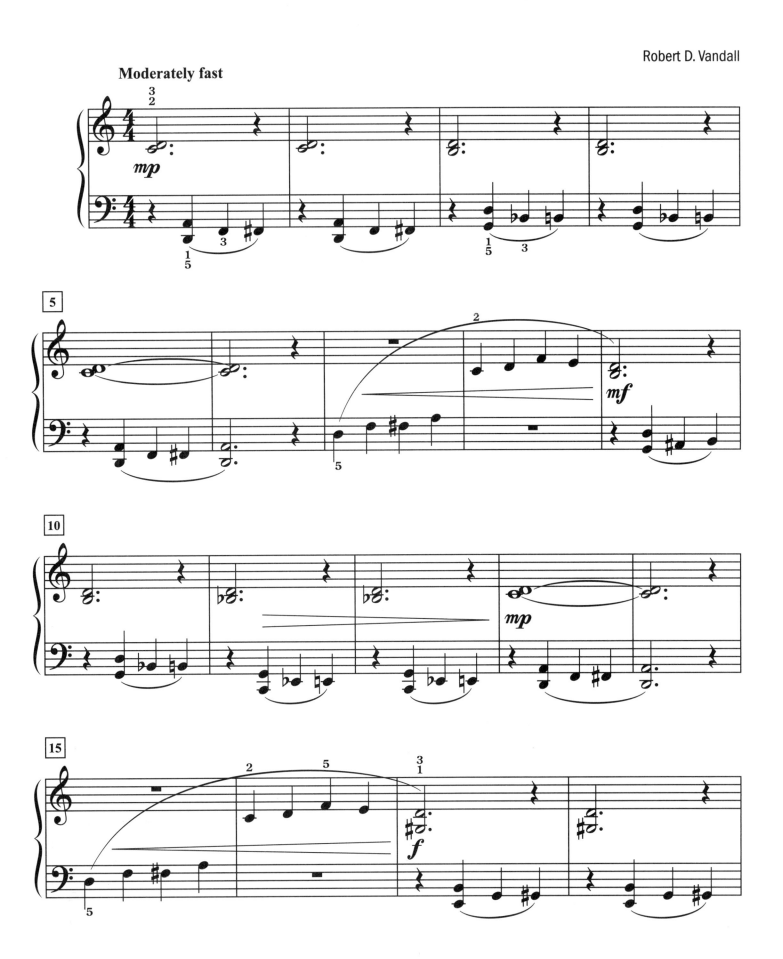

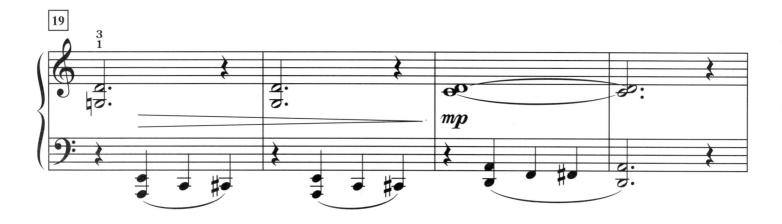

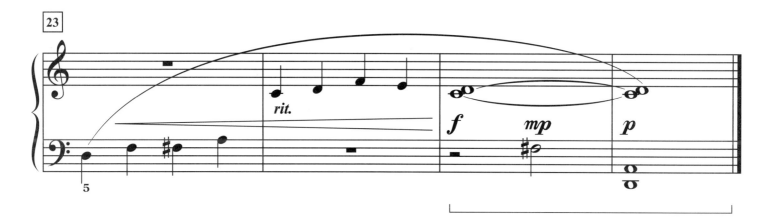

Hammock Blues

Robert D. Vandall

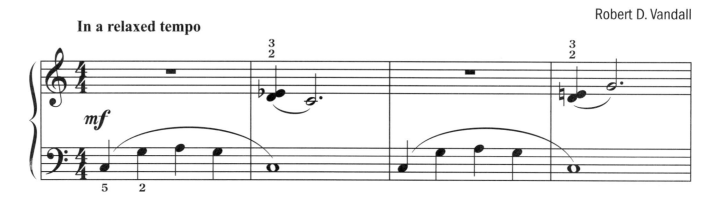

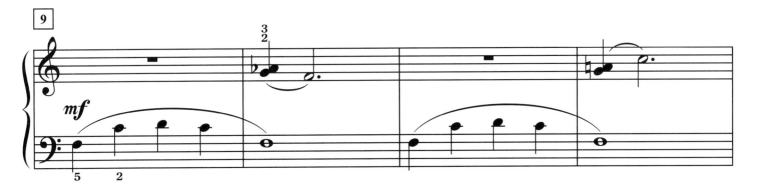

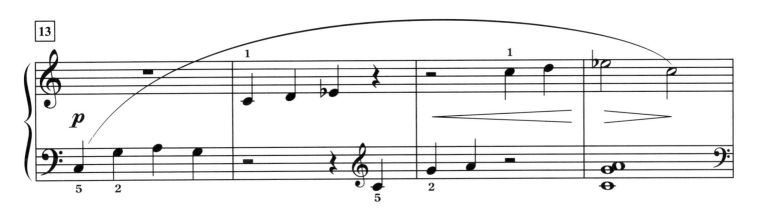

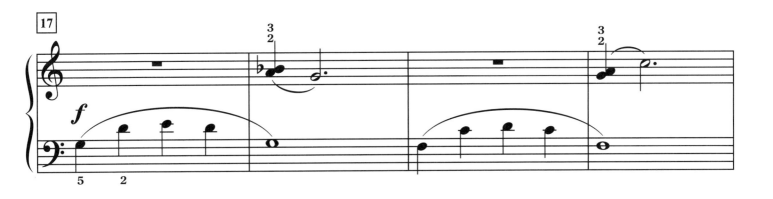

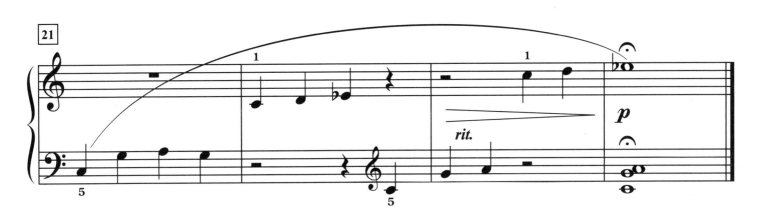

Stepping Stones

Robert D. Vandall

Two Hands Boogie

Robert D. Vandall

Stomping Five

Robert D. Vandall

Hurry Up!

Robert D. Vandall

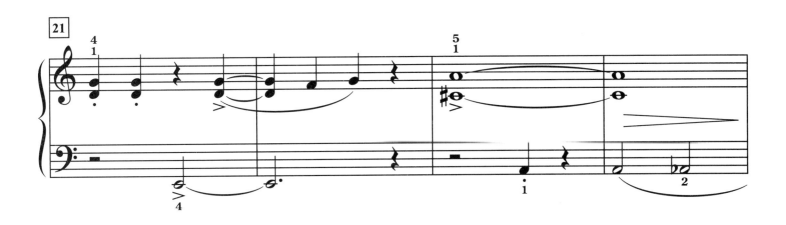

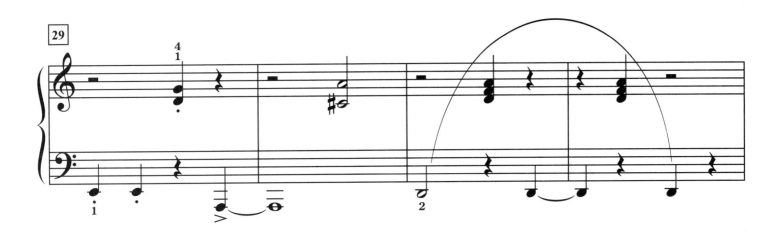

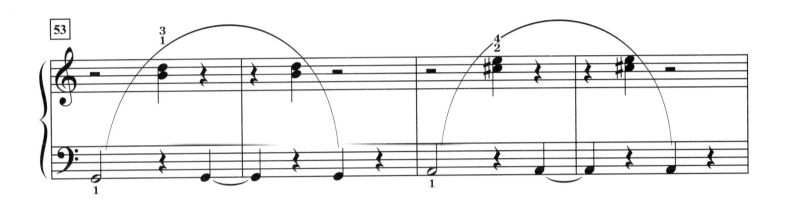

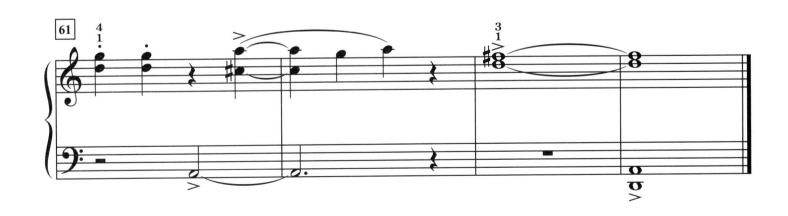

Sidewalk Strut

Robert D. Vandall

**Moderately fast;
strongly accented and rhythmic**

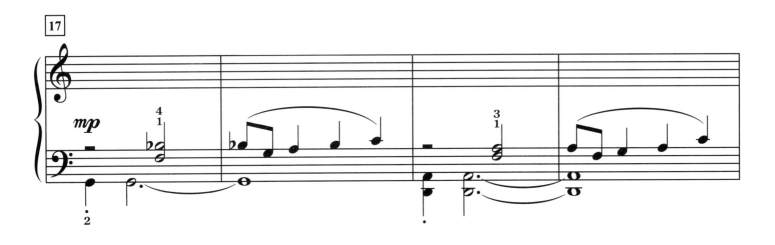

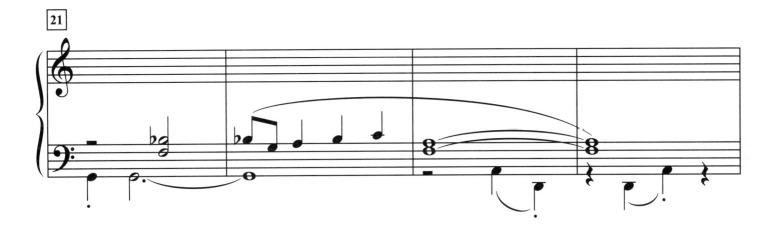

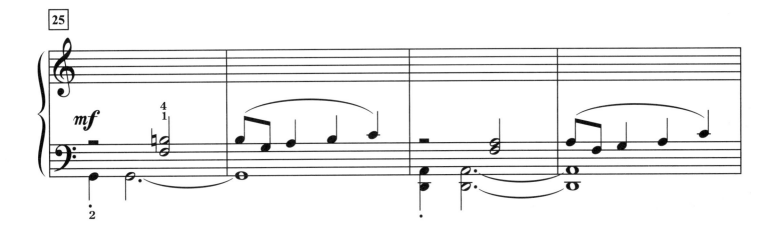

D. C. al Fine

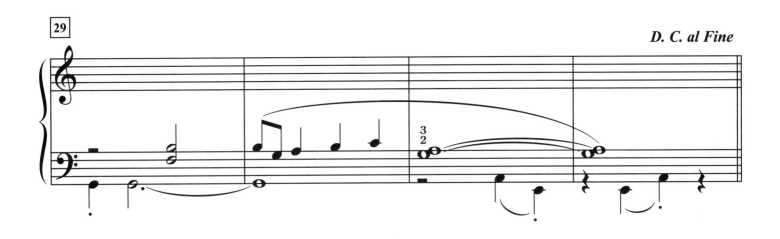

Blues Jaunt

Robert D. Vandall

Harmony Rag

Robert D. Vandall

Moderately fast

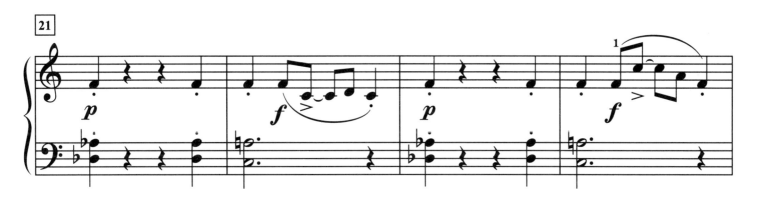

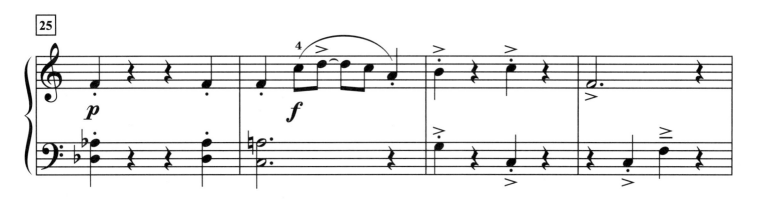